16.

I FOUND THIS SHIRT

Ian McMillan

I FOUND THIS SHIRT

poems and prose from the centre

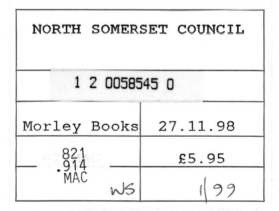
CARCANET

First published in 1998 by
Carcanet Press Limited
4th Floor, Conavon Court
12-16 Blackfriars Street
Manchester M3 5BQ

A CIP catalogue record for this book
is available from the British Library
ISBN 1 85754 336 X

The publisher acknowledges financial assistance
from the Arts Council of England

Set in 10pt Bookman by Bryan Williamson, Frome
Printed and bound in England by SRP Ltd, Exeter

Acknowledgements

The Wide Skirt, Poems for National Poetry Day,
The Daily Telegraph, The Barnsley Chronicle,
Fourth Column (BBC Radio 4), *The Afternoon Shift*
(BBC Radio 4), *Live From the Crypt* (BBC Radio 4)
Perfect Pitch.

The Cautionary Tales were commissioned by
the South Bank Centre.

Contents

Introduction

Welcome to *I Found This Shirt*; I hope you enjoy it. It's not really a book of poems or stories; I want it to be a book about what it's like to be a writer in Barnsley in the nineties. There are poems in here, and columns written for newspapers and the radio, and poems for children including a set of new Cautionary Tales written to be performed with musicians. Most of the words in here were written to be said out loud, so please do say them out loud!

I'd Better Not

A man leaned over to a man
In a pub and said, in a voice,
'I used to be 37
But now I'm 51'

And that's how the years go,
In handfuls, like somebody
Is almost at the end
Of a bag of crisps

And they tip the bag up
And it's as though they're
Drinking crisps. That's
How the years go.

Today, one of my daughters
Is 13, and one of my daughters
Is 11. My son is 8. I'm 40.
My wife is 41. My dad is 77.

My mam is 74. That is how
The years go. Very bleached,
Is the grass on that coast;
I was going to explain that,

Fill you in. I just had to
Answer the phone and somebody
Asked me if I was a photographer.
Once, one of my daughters

Was 1, one of my daughters
Wasn't born, my son wasn't
Born, I was 28, my wife was
29, my dad was 65,

My mam was 62, and I took
A photograph. Very bleached,
Is the grass on that coast.
That is how the years go.

What Happened

What happened was this: I was at a festival in the north of England, reading my poems out to an audience in a town hall. I was on with an excellent singer/songwriter but he was a bit loud for some of the crowd so they went out when he was on and came back when I was on. I was a bit quiet for some of the crowd so they went out when I was on and came back when he was on. It was like performing at a wedding reception. In the interval I mentioned to the organiser that I had to get the 6.40 am train from Skipton the next day, so there and then, outside the town hall in the golden light of a summer's evening, she rang for a taxi on her mobile. 'SIX O'CLOCK,' she said in a loud voice, as loud as the singer/songwriter's songs, 'YOU HAVE TO BE THERE AT SIX O'CLOCK IN THE MORNING'.

After the gig (I call them gigs to pretend that poetry really is the new rock and roll) I went back to the House of the Organiser's Friend to stay the night. I knew that I was at the House of the Organiser's Friend because I had told the Organiser I was allergic to dogs and cats and therefore the Friend would have no dogs or cats. We went into the darkened house with the Friend and the Friend's Mother. A large dog bounded up. A cat purred round my legs. 'Do you like animals?' said the Organiser's Friend.

We chatted. I kept patting my pocket to make sure my inhaler was still there. The Organiser's Friend's Husband turned up, fresh from a convention of garden railway enthusiasts in Norfolk. We talked about garden railways for a while as I patted my pocket to make sure my inhaler was still there and the cat wound round my legs and the dog slept happily at my feet. I went to bed, waking every half hour thinking it was six o'clock.

At four thirty I got up and sat on the windowsill looking out of the window. A horse clopped by. An aeroplane buzzed distantly. I gazed, thinking of garden railways and loud singer/songwriters. I must have nodded off. Suddenly it was six am and there was no taxi. Then it was ten past six and there was no taxi. I patted my pocket and next to my inhaler was the taxi firm's card. I rang them. 'He's on his way but he's lost,' said a voice; 'Where are you?'

'I don't know,' I said, 'I came here in the dark.' 'What's the name of the street?' said the taxi man, patiently. 'I'm not on a street,' I said, getting my inhaler out. 'Can you see anything out of the window that might help my driver?' he said. 'A horse,' I said. He rang off.

I didn't know what to do. The 6.40 train loomed. The taxi man was driving around North Yorkshire looking for a horse. I rang back. 'There's a railway in the garden,' I said. 'That doesn't help me, friend,' he said.

There was nothing else to do: I had to wake the Friend of the Organiser up so that she could give directions to the taxi man. I wandered around the huge house. The dog growled in his sleep. I knocked on various doors saying the word 'Hello' very quietly. I wanted to laugh. I knew that I had to record a piece for Radio 4's *Fourth Column* later that day. I knew that I had to make it for that train. I opened a door saying 'Hello'. The Organiser's Friend's Mother sat up briefly then slumped back into sleep. I opened another door saying 'Hello'. The Organiser's Friend and the Organiser's Friend's Husband were deeply asleep. 'Hello. Hello. Hello.' The Organiser's Friend swam up from sleep. 'What's wrong?' she mumbled. 'It's Ian,' I said, 'I don't know where I am.'

She looked at me across the room. Her eyes were beginning to focus. 'It's okay, Ian, you're safe. You're with us.' Somewhere outside, the taxi was driving in circles.

My Dog

April is the Cruellest Month
might seem like a strange name for a dog,
and sometimes I think it is
when I'm shouting her name
on the high moors
in the driving wind.

'April is the Cruellest Month!'
I shout,
'April is the Cruellest Month'
and my dog runs up to me,
barking, wagging her tail,
and I feel slightly, ever so slightly
embarrassed.

But then when people say
as they walk by me
on the high moors
in the driving wind,
'Can a month bark?'
'Can April wag its tail?'
I swell with pride
because my dog's name
is image, and metaphor, and poetry.

So,
'April is the Cruellest Month'
I shout, and
'April is the Cruellest Month'
and the words roll round my mouth
like Easter Eggs in a Shopping Basket
which is the name of my cat.

Finger Trouble

This isn't a column, really. It's a letter of apology. Sorry, Steve. Sorry, pal. Sorry about the finger and everything. Sorry about the years in the wilderness. Sorry.

OK, I'd better start at the beginning. The late Seventies. I'd finished at college and I was working on a building site because that was the sort of thing you did in those days. I was a labourer, which meant I was the lowest of the low. Everybody else on the site looked like they should be in The Chippendales, and I looked like a slug in a vest. I read the *Guardian* in the cabin, and they set fire to it with a cigarette lighter. I rodded drains with a man called Crackerjack who was slightly deaf. 'Let me know when the stuff's coming through,' he would shout, and he never heard me. He'd chase me, mucky faced, up the site with a shovel.

I enjoyed it though; I loved it. It felt like Real Life, after all those years at college. I used to wax lyrical about it to Steve at night in the pub. Steve was one of my old school pals; we shared artistic leanings. I was a poet, he was a cellist. I went on about the blokes on the building site like they were straight out of Rabelais. Crackerjack, Arthur, Vinny, Mountie became legendary characters, larger than life, larger than anything.

I was called into the office by the ganger. I was a bit scared because the only other time I'd been in the ganger's office I'd had something in my eye. I was hoping for an afternoon off because my eye was watering tumultuously, but he just lifted my eyelid up with a six-inch nail and flicked out the offending thing in my eye with a razor-sharp finger. 'Could be a bit of ash from your paper,' he said with a grin. So now I was in the ganger's office again, and he was grinning again. 'Normally I've not got much time for students,' he said, 'but you're okay. You can take a joke. And there's plenty of work on, so I was wondering if you'd got any mates who might like to join this madhouse . . .' Sorry Steve. That's how I got you into it, that fateful moment in the ganger's office.

That night in the pub I told Steve. We were trying to drink tequilas because we were both in a Malcolm Lowry phase, so consequently we could hardly speak. I tried to convey to him that he

16

would be the lowest of the low. He tried to convey happiness. We smiled and chinked our glasses together.

The next day he brought his *Guardian* as well. They set fire to both of them. 'What do you do then, love?' said Joe, as he drank his raw egg mixed with brandy. 'Play the cello,' said Steve, miming a few quick notes on an imaginary instrument. 'Then sweet Jesus help us all,' said Joe. Outside, the ganger came up. He looked at Steve. Oh, Steve, pal, if I could only turn time back! 'Can you drive?' he asked. Steve nodded, miming driving. Miming was his big thing. Other ex-students our age thought it was funny. 'We need another dumper driver,' said the ganger, 'off you go!'

Do you remember it, Steve, the bright yellow dumper? Do you recall that you had to drive down to where Vinny was, with a load of bags of cement that me and Crackerjack chucked in? Do you remember that Crackerjack said, 'I hear you play the cello. You can teach me which end to blow it'? Do you remember the bright blue day, the jolting drive down the site? Steve, I'm sorry.

The dumper disappeared down the site. Me and Arthur followed, slowly, to stack some bricks at the side of the house Vinny was working on. The day was bright and blue.

We heard Steve shout; we saw him leap off the dumper and mime extreme pain. We saw him waving his finger about like he was trying to swat a wasp. We saw Vinny pointing. We saw the ganger running. Maybe that was the day the Seventies lost their innocence for me, because I'd always been an innocent fat lad until then.

He'd broken his finger, of course. He had a couple of weeks off, and then a day a week physiotherapy. He had to give up the cello. He became a man who made stage sets. Sorry, Steve. Innocence always goes, but it doesn't always go with a crack of bone.

Then, a few weeks ago, I saw another old pal in the supermarket car park. We talked over old times, and he told me about Steve. 'He's teaching the cello now,' he said, as he packed bulging bags into the car, 'in the Orkneys.'

The Orkneys; that's a long way from Barnsley, Steve. A long way from Crackerjack and Vinny. A long way from a bright yellow dumper on a bright blue day. Do you stand there miming your hat blowing off in a high Orkney wind? I hope so. Have a tequila on me. And don't drive anything down a bumpy track.

Not much chance of that, in the Orkneys.

17

Boxing Day

By now the kids are crying
from lack of sleep
and the toys are piled up
in a broken heap
and the parents are crying
hollow-eyed
and the turkey's been nibbled
down just a small part of one side . . .

And Christmas Day
is slipping away
like a fat boy down a slide in the park.
And Christmas Day
is falling over
like a drunken stumble in the dark . . .

But never mind,
never mind,
Boxing Day's
not far behind . . .

Never mind,
never mind,
Boxing Day's here
to screw up your mind . . .

Boxing Day's like walking through the arctic
with a bit of cold turkey and a paper hat.
Boxing Day's like falling in the snow.

A New Christmas Tradition

Christmas is a time for traditions, and I think now that it's time to start a new one, at just after half-past six on Christmas Day. Christmas traditions can be started just like that, as you know: the Christmas tree was, and the baubles on the Christmas tree were. Prince Albert, or someone, just decided that they should be part of Christmas and suddenly they were!

Our image of Santa comes from the poem 'Twas the night before Christmas', and our image of Santa was strengthened by the illustrations for that poem.

A Christmas tradition started and accepted. Just like that.

So tonight, here on *Live from the Crypt*, we're going to start a new Christmas Day tradition with the aid of this MILK BOTTLE and this STICK. Improbable? Well, have a listen to this . . .

(Rattles milk bottle on stick)

It's just a milk bottle rattling on a stick, but for the purposes of our tradition it's going to sound like the Shivering Teeth of the Shepherds. The shivering teeth of the shepherds as they sat in the fields guarding their sheep just before the angels appeared to them.

Tell you what: I'll rattle the milk bottle on the stick, and you say: 'What's that?'

And I'll say: 'It's the shivering teeth of the shepherds as they waited for the angels.'

Let's try it!

Self Portrait

Face a red planet
smudged by glasses, he's
slumped in the bus seat

As the sun rises, illuminating
the little bits of whisker
he's missed, iron filings

On the nodding red planet.
How small his hands are.
How Elvis his hair is.

He may be a collapsing balloon,
chins folded like dough,
sun reflects on the glasses.

Communication

The Summer seems a long time away, now that the nights are cold and black, but a couple of things happened to me on warm beaches last August that seemed to explain something profound, in the way that moments on beaches often can. If you doubt that, think about the time you wandered to the sea and came back to where your parents were and they'd gone, moved miles away down the beach and you stood there crying in your trunks and really they were in the same place and it was you who'd moved down the shore. Image for loss of innocence or what? Or the time you looked up from a sandwich and saw two donkeys making love. Image for loss of innocence or what?

The papers are full of communication these days, or lack of it. Parents aren't communicating with children, teachers aren't communicating with parents, politicians aren't communicating with each other or with us. Society is breaking down; we're all coming out of the sea further towards the sewerage works than when we went in, or we're all picking the frisky donkey that wants to throw us off and run down the sand in search of a soulmate.

I was on a beach near Eyemouth in Scotland, and even the name of the place seemed to be significant. Eye. Mouth. Communication writ large. My little lad had finished his bottle of Ribena and had written a message to go in it. It was simple enough. Hello. My name is Andrew. Will you be my penpal? And then the address and postcode, painstakingly. We wandered to the sea's edge. The tide was boisterous and the beach was crowded. Andrew rolled his arm like Pete Townshend used to do, and flung the bottle into the sea. Then a strange thing happened. The bottle went out about six feet, and then came straight back again, but not straight to Andrew's feet, to the feet of a little boy standing next to us. I thought he'd laugh and give it back to Andrew, but he didn't. Amazingly, he picked it up, he looked at it in excitement, he held it up to the wide Eyemouth sky and whooped with delight at the sight of the message inside. He hadn't seen Andrew throw it in. Andrew threw it in about a yard from him and the boy hadn't seen him do it. The boy passed the bottle to his dad and the dad opened it. He read it. Hello. My name is

Andrew . . . the waves crashed in and the boy folded the message and ran up to where his mum was reading *The Scotsman*.

Isn't that what communication ends up being? You fling your message out to the wide foaming oceans and nobody notices you sending it, not even the person who eventually finds it, who was standing next to you the whole time. In these times of moral panic (watch the eye, watch the mouth) we tell each other things about the fabric of society splitting like a fat boy's swimming cossy but nobody's listening, not even the people who are giving the message.

A couple of days later, on the same beach, we found a tub of plastic letters with magnets on; the sort you stick on a fridge. At the time it didn't seem like an unusual find, which shows how out of the rut you actually do get on holiday. My oldest girl wanted to make THIS ISN'T A FRIDGE out of the letters and spread them across the sand; she's a surrealist, like her dad. She sorted the letters into piles. Inevitably, there were plenty of some, few of others. She could make THIS IS A FRIDGE GELWAV.

THIS IS A FRIDGE GELWAV sounded pretty good to me, but my daughter wasn't enough of a surrealist for the GELWAV, so she put it back in the tub and spread the other letters out. THIS IS A FRIDGE it said on the beach. Profound: you can only use the words you've got. That's what communication is. The beach is a fridge. Black is white. The person who's got all the letters in the tub is in charge, and that person can make whatever words they want. Can't they, Mr Murdoch?

See you on the sands next year. I'll be the one averting my eyes from the donkeys.

Cautionary Tale for Elderly Relatives

Note: this is a chant for performer and
audience to interact with

Grandma's fallen down the stairs
Oh no
Grandma's fallen down the stairs

Grandma's fallen down the stairs
Oh no
Grandma's fallen down the stairs

Grandad's climbing up a tree
Dear me
Grandad's climbing up a tree

Grandad's climbing up a tree
Dear me
Grandad's climbing up a tree

Elderly relatives
flying through the air
Elderly relatives
everywhere
Elderly relatives
please watch out
Elderly relatives
scream and shout

Uncle's jumping off a bus
Look out!
Uncle's jumping off a bus

Uncle's jumping off a bus
Look out!
Uncle's jumping off a bus

Auntie's slicing up ham
watch it
Auntie's slicing up ham

Elderly relatives
taking lots of chances
Elderly relatives
accident dances
Elderly relatives
dangerous
Elderly relatives
make a fuss

Great Grandad's swinging off a rope
some hope
Great Grandad's swinging off a rope

Great Grandad's swinging off a rope
some hope
Great Grandad's swinging off a rope

Great Grandma's gonna break her neck
flipping heck
Great Grandma's gonna break her neck

Great Grandma's gonna break her neck
flipping heck
Great Grandma's gonna break her neck

Elderly relatives
acting like fools
don't they know
the elderly rules?
Elderly relatives
shouldn't be allowed
Elderly relatives
a frightening crowd!

Stationery: The New Lingerie

Some people linger outside bookshops, gazing at the gleaming covers and seeing themselves living in a fictional world, or at least a world less complicated and dreary than their own. Some people hang around lingerie shops, seeing a glamorous universe and oceans of endless possibility in red G-strings and black stockings. I pity these people. You'll find me at the stationery shop window. You can keep your Rough Guides to Morocco and your camisole tops; give me paper clips and hole punchers, tippex and bulldog clips; tiny totems of the humanising march of history.

We're supposed to be in the paperless world; our offices are meant to hum like fridges rather than rustle like paper shops. The light is meant to be subdued, the words are meant to be on the screens, the waste baskets are meant to be almost empty, containing just an odd bit of plastic and the bag your sandwiches came in. As we all know, this isn't the case. I was in an office the other day. An office full of people; modern people, folks *d'aujourd' hui*, and this wasn't a paperless zone, not by any means. There were rubber bands, paper clips, pencils in pots, bits of paper, post-it notes, envelopes with things really scribbled on the back of them, pencil cases like ones you have at school, and great huge waste bins overflowing with paper, foaming with paper, bursting with paper.

As always my kids were the ones in the front line, the ones who alerted me to the survival of stationery in the foothills of the millennium. When I go shopping with them they don't want to stop first at the record shop or the burger bar or the trendy clothes shop or the bookshop. They're straight to the stationery shop and they're diving in amongst the folders and the rubbers and the A4 paper. My son got all sorts of stuff last Christmas, but the thing he liked best was a pencil tin that looks like it's covered with baked beans. He loved it. All his mates have got 'em. And pencil cases that look like crisp packets. I held up his pencil tin with baked beans on it late on Boxing Day afternoon when the beer and sleeplessness were just kicking in and attempted to define some form of cultural movement using words like post-modernism and zeitgeist; the other people in the room looked at me for a few seconds then turned back to a black and white film. I fell into a fitful sleep, dribbling down at least two of my chins. Since then, though, I've been thinking about the survival, indeed the rehabilitation, of stationery. Somehow, in a really fundamental way (and I haven't had any beer, and I slept really well last night) the computer has been defeated by the pencil sharpener, and there's not a thing Bill Gates can do about it. It's a bit like the First World War: all that carnage, all that horror, all that death and destruction, all those forces beyond the average soldier to comprehend, but what does he do: he personalises his trench, hangs daft signs up, keeps letters from his wife under his pillow and a lucky fob watch in his pocket. He's saying: you can keep your inexorable march of history, this is me and this is my lucky fob watch.

And that's why stationery is so beautiful in the computer age: it reminds us that we are human, and not just things that look at screens and press mice. Pencils can be chewed, tippex can be spilled, paper clips can be straightened out and yellow post-it notes can be stuck over your glasses to make you look like somebody with bright yellow glasses on. And if that isn't all cutting edge and postmodern, I don't know what is. See you by the top shelf: the one with the different sized envelopes and the five-year diaries.

Cautionary Tale for Rhyming Poets

Ian McMillan
was a poet
whose poems
occasionally rhymed.
Sometimes they did
and sometimes they didn't
and nobody seemed to care.

Sometimes his poems
were free as sweet papers
blowing in the breeze

and they were sometimes as noisy
as wallpaper scrapers
scratching the leaves
off the Autumn trees . . .

But
Ian McMillan
was a poet
whose poems
occasionally rhymed.
Sometimes they did
and sometimes they didn't
and nobody seemed to bother.

And then he got bitten
by the Rhyming Bat
that flies through the forest at night
and rhyme began
to seep into his poems
before the morning light . . .

Because the Rhyming Bat
is a Deadly Bat
whose bite leaves you desperate for rhyme
and you rhyme all the time
and you rhyme and you rhyme
and your poems go on rhyming all day
and the rhymes won't stop coming
like some incessant drumming
and the rhyming is rhyming to stay.

Ian McMillan
was a poet
whose poems occasionally rhymed.
Sometimes they did
and sometimes they didn't
and nobody seemed to mind

nobody seemed to mind . . .

Nobody seemed to mind . . .

MORAL:

Try not to get bitten
by the Rhyming Bat
or that will be
the end of that.

Ian McMillanish Things

People are queuing up to make Ian McMillanish things happen to me. They see me coming and they say to each other in their small voices, 'Here He Comes. Here he comes now. He expects things to be strange. He expects Ian McMillanish things to happen. Fulfil him. Fulfil him.'

So I was in this pub in Elland, near Huddersfield, waiting to talk to a group of librarians at a place called Bertie's Banqueting Rooms, and that is not the strange thing. And I was sitting in the corner of the pub nursing a half of something friendly, there was a big TV in the corner of the pub and American football was happening on it, silently. The pub was empty apart from me and the landlady and a man who looked like James Robertson Justice playing a ferry steward. There was a long emptiness, the American football game continued in silence, and I thought, Some-thing Ian McMillanish is about to happen. And it did.

The landlady reached over and gave a carrier to James Robertson Justice playing a ferry steward, and she said, 'Here are your clocks', and the Ian McMillanish thing was beginning to happen, beginning to run its inevitable course like a wind-up toy. James Robertson Justice seemed pleased. 'Great,' he said. 'Clocks.' And his dog, a big black one, leaped up at the bar, and the man shouted, 'Bad boy! Not bones! Clocks! Not to eat! Not bones!' And the Ian McMillanish thing was proceeding normally, and I sat in the corner of the pub and let it happen to me.

The dog carried on jumping up and James Robertson Justice kept telling it off. The phone rang behind the bar, and the landlady answered it. She turned to James and said, 'It's your mother' and he turned his eyes to heaven and picked up the phone. The dog carried on leaping up, barking for joy at the thought of a carrier of clocks that might have been bones.

'Yes mother,' said James Robertson Justice as a ferry steward, 'Yes, I know all about Morecambe. Yes, I know I'll have to get you out of Morecambe and I'm doing the best I can but there isn't a bus till Tuesday.' He was about to carry on when the dog leaped on the bar and got a clock in its mouth. It ran round the bar with the clock in its mouth, and it wasn't just that the clock was in the dog's mouth, the clock was stuck in the dog's mouth. It looked like an awful ornament. A dog with a clock in its mouth. And I sat there in the pub in Elland near Huddersfield with the Ian McMillanish thing happening around me and it was as though I was in the middle of a strange Ian McMillan storm. I was in the eye of it. And then the dog began to bark, and that became the most Ian McMillanish thing of all, because as the dog was barking with the clock in its mouth and the clock in its mouth was muffling the bark, it sounded like the dog was saying Clock. Clock Clock went the dog. Clock Clock.

And when I got home I told my wife about it, about my theory that Ian McMillanish things were happening to me, and she didn't believe me. 'You make them up,' she said. 'But I don't,' I said, pointing out that she was ironing on a table instead of an ironing board, and that our two gerbils were standing side by side watching her. 'That's not Ian McMillanish,' she said, 'The ironing board's broken and the gerbils often sit in a line. They're not watching me iron. I doubt if they can see that far.'

So maybe Ian McMillanish things aren't happening to me. Maybe if anybody else had gone in that pub that night the man who looked like James Robertson Justice as a ferry steward wouldn't have been there and the dog wouldn't have run round with a clock in its mouth saying clock clock. But that night I was woken up by the phone ringing, and I went downstairs and it was the middle of the night, and I answered the phone, and a voice said 'Is that the Royal Oak?' and I said 'I'm not a tree' and the voice said, and I swear this is true, 'I think I've heard your voice on the radio' and I said 'Thanks very much' and I put the phone down because I knew that if I'd carried on talking an Ian McMillanish thing would have happened to me. And before I went back to bed I looked at the gerbils and they were sitting in a line looking at me. And in the distant Barnsley night a black dog should have gone Clock Clock, but it didn't. That would have been silly.

Martian Caution

(Note to Ben: this poem is meant to be about someone who eats a banana and slowly turns into a banana; I don't know if that can be implied through the music)

Note: parts of this poem have been translated from the Martian, but mostly it's in the original language.

CHORUS:
Ick necknock threcknock necknock
griz!

So kockleck throcklek banana
biz!

Ick necknock threcknock necknock
griz!

So kockleck throcklek banana
biz!

Sendri masonta masonta Tesco   Olytona groploppy
                                                pushtrolley   pushtrolley
noscnock trop plop fruit and vegetables   Rushtrolley
                                                pushtrolley treb treb treb

Sendri throckleck up blob blob blib banana tower
                                Pushtrolley
                                Rushtrolley

glob bal;b noportiniung banana 23,000. More banana: 24,000.
                                        More banana: 25,000.

CHORUS:

Ick necknock threcknock necknock
griz!

So kockleck throcklek banana
biz!

Etc . . .

Se

So here I am, with my head stuck through the ceiling. Let's look at it another way. So here I am, with my head stuck through the floor. I'm in limbo. I'm like a broken lift, jammed between haberdashery and soft furnishings.

I'm on a quest for the perfect attic, and the perfect attic is proving harder to find than the golden fleece, or even the tin fleece, which is the sort of thing you think you'd find in an attic. I asked around, friends and acquaintances, people behind me in the supermarket queue, people at the next table in the pub, 'Can I look in your attic? Can I look in your dusty, fusty, musty attic?' And they'd look at me with a look reserved for someone who asked for a pack of Betamax videos and they'd say, 'Well, we used to have an attic, but now it's the kid's bedroom or the playroom or the study.' I began to despair of finding a traditional attic like the ones you have in fiction. You know the ones I mean: the young lad, perhaps in shorts and a school cap, climbs up the rickety rickety stairs to find the cricket pads his dad had in the summer before the war. He pushes open the hatch to the attic and clambers in, wiping ancient cobwebs from his face. The only light is from a dusty casement window, so the boy can't see his dad's cricket pads, which of course are a metaphor for lost innocence. The boy pulls a trunk towards him, opens it, carefully moves the golden or tin fleece out of the way, and finds a pile of old family photo albums. He opens one and looks through it. There's a picture of his mam and dad, standing with a stranger; well, almost a stranger. Except it's Uncle Bert, long lost Uncle Bert who went out for a bag of chips on the day BBC2 started and never came back, causing a family scandal. And the young lad is determined to find him. And that's fiction, and that's the kind of romantic glow we've got around attics. That attic would be a Gold Medal, Five Star, DeLuxe attic, and I don't think they exist any more. Instead of pre-war cricket pads you get posters of Boyzone and beds covered in cuddly toys.

I had one more go. I went to see my mam and dad, and said, 'Can I look in your attic,' and they said, 'We haven't got an attic, you know we haven't got an attic, we've got a loft', and I thought about how language really determines the kind of house you've got: That's not a conservatory, it's a sun loggia, but that's another story. So I get the steps out of the garage, musing on how with some people the garage has taken over the past-gathering functions of an attic, and I climbed up, and stuck my head through the floor, or through the ceiling, and I couldn't see a thing, so I switched on the Simpson's torch my lad had got for Christmas, and I shone it round the room and it was like, well it was like . . . I'll tell you what it was like: it was like an art installation depicting a calm sea at night. There was nothing left in the loft except the stuff they put down to insulate against heat loss, rolls of it, gleaming yellowy in the light of the Simpson's torch. And I thought: how Nineties, how *fin-de-siecle*. I'm not a boy in shorts looking for his dad's cricket pads, I'm a forty something with a Simpson's torch gazing into nothing.

So here I am with my head through the floor, or through the ceiling, reflecting on the failure of my quest to find the perfect attic. Except, except: in the light of this Simpson's torch, doesn't that insulating stuff look like the Golden Fleece? I think it does!

Tuesdays and Wednesdays

I imagined it would be a sad place
The last room before death

A place of tears and silence
A slow dwindling to the last breath.

It isn't: it's a place of affirmation
That *now* is important, not the hereafter

It taught me a lot: how to listen,
How to take each story as fresh and new,

How we can all teach each other a lesson
How the telling of a life makes a life true:

And it confirmed what I'd suspected all along
That everyone's artistic in a personal way

Art's what makes us human and our song
Sings from the morning to the close of the day.

Maybe it was the heat. Even in my loud shirt I felt like I was walking round in a chip pan. It felt like I was standing warming my bum at the fire in the middle of August. It was as hot as it used to be in the Tennis Ball Factory before the health and safety men came round and made them put fans in.

Wait a minute: I shouldn't be talking about chip pans and warm bums and sweltering Tennis Ball factories; this is 1997; we've got a new Labour government or a new New Labour Government and the future is stretching out like an unlicked lolly. The chip pans have had their warm bums relegated to the Tennis Ball Factory of history and my loud shirt is a reflection of how confident we feel.

Except I'm still stuck in the past, literally, as I find it hard to drag my hurting feet another yard round this vast Heritage site. It's two hours from Barnsley to the Heritage Site, two hours from a land of shut down pits and terraced houses to another land of shut down pits and terraced houses except this one you have to pay for. Two hours up a motorway as hot as the pans of boiling milk my mam used to make coffee with, as hot as the top deck of the 37 bus used to be as it rolled into Barnsley on a red hot Saturday morning in the Sixties, full of women off to have their hair permed and men coming home from the pit, all smoking like bonfires do on November 6th. This heat must be getting to me. The heat of history. The future is a cool, cool icebox and I'm here sweating like a piggy.

This is what we did at the Heritage Site: we put our hands in our pockets and handed over our credit cards for a good caning. We walked through the Old Heritage School that looked just like the one I was in in Rotherham the other week. We walked through the street of Authentic Heritage Terraced Houses that looked just like Cross Street in Great Houghton where my mam was born, and oddly enough looked just like Cross Street does now. Give or take the odd satellite dish. We queued for an authentic Heritage tram with other hot people. A man who looked like a child's drawing of a Grandad said, to no one in particular, 'This is great', and the odd thing was that he meant it, and the odder thing was that he'd lived through it, and here he was saying that this kit version of History, History Lite, was Great. I felt all out of kilter. I felt like a potato about to be mashed by my auntie in her stiflingly hot kitchen with the Yorkshire range and my Uncle Charlie sat there like a washed-out waxwork, tanned off-white by years and years down Houghton Main as History washed past him, overground.

The Eighties felt like the heyday of History as Heritage, of pits shutting and mining museums opening, of sanitised versions of the last couple of centuries being accepted as The Real Thing, of young actors with dodgy accents telling you their story of how they went to the mill at the age of twelve, as you elbowed past them to get to the Gift Shop. All that felt and stunk like the Eighties, that awful decade, not these brand-new shiny cool air-conditioned Nineties that'll help you across the street and make sure you get a seat on the bus.

The sweat poured off my face at the Heritage Site. My children bickered and fought and wouldn't talk to the nice actors who were pretending to be shop workers and people sitting in houses. I had an ice cream that dripped spectacularly down my loud shirt. My wife shouted and my wife very rarely shouts. Toddlers were crying, couples were arguing, even the old feller who'd said 'This is great' earlier was to be seen frowning and fanning himself with a postcard in the late afternoon sun. We toiled back to the car up a steep hill. You could have fried an egg on the bonnet if that was your idea of a good time. An actor could have leaped out and told us a tale about how she went to an egg-frying factory at the age of twelve and we couldn't have cared less.

The future is nice and cool and we're all hot and sweaty. The past was hot and sweaty and a struggle and not nice most of the time and not this cleaned-up version. It's a simple enough premise; but now the future is here, it's been voted in, I just hope it'll allow the past to still be there, hot as a steelworks in late July, hotter than the top deck of an Authentic Heritage Tram.

Fried egg, anyone? Authentic Heritage Fried Egg, anyone?

Home Support

It is mid-July, 1997. It is hot.
Barnsley are in the Premier League,
and in my head our season
is laid out as simple as an Underground Map,
or a child's drawing of the solar system.
Mid-July, a pre-season friendly
against Doncaster. The start of something
and one of my daughters is coming to Doncaster
on her own for the first time on the bus
to meet me to go to the match. As the bus
rolls into the bus station I see her red shirt
upstairs, and she waves, and my heart breaks

for her, and me, and her red shirt with 21 TINKLER
on the back, and the bus driver who is a Middlesbrough fan,
and the other people who tumble off the bus in their red shirts
with the season laid out in their heads simple and lovely
as a map of the solar system or a child's drawing
of the Underground, and the Greek bus station toilet attendant
who knows me and shouts PREMIER LEAGUE, but
mostly it breaks for her, and me, and her red shirt.

Still, it's July. It's hot. We meet Chris and Duncan
and we try to go into a pub even though my daughter's
a bit young and a man in a suit says Sorry, Home Support Only.
And my heart breaks

for her, and me, and her red shirt, and the Home Support
who cheer Doncaster and whose season is laid out simple
as a serving suggestion, or a child's drawing of a football team,
but mostly it breaks for her and me.

We get a taxi home, which seems extravagant, but I think
of the Greek toilet attendant and I shout PREMIER LEAGUE
on our path as we walk into the house, father and daughter, red
shirt, hot night, Home Support, season laid out in our heads
simple and lovely as a football programme, simple and lovely
as a penalty kick, a well-taken corner.

Premier Days

I've always woken up before the alarm clock; take that as a metaphor if you like, read it as an image of the ever-watchful writer, the eyes and ears of the tribe, but it's just a fact. I always wake up before the alarm clock. Except once.

Premiership fever was at boiling point last Summer in Barnsley; every car that passed had a sticker in the back, every time you turned to the back page of the *Barnsley Chronicle* you saw the smiling face of yet another close-season signing: Georgi Hristov, the bewildered-looking werewolf from Eastern Europe who was going to be our Juninho; Eric Tinkler, the huge South African who was simply going to stop them getting past him in midfield; and Lars Leese, the German goalkeeper, tall as a basketball player, who said he used to follow Barnsley on German TV. They all made us smile.

My job as poet-in-residence at the club was part of the maelstrom. The idea came to me and my mate, local headteacher and Barnsley fanatic Julian Wroe, in the Royal Oak in Wombwell one quiet Wednesday night. I'd worked a lot around Barnsley as a poet-in-the-community and being the poet at the football club seemed like a logical progression. We agreed to hold back on the publicity for a while and then do a proper press release at the start of the next season; at that time we weren't even promoted, and several nail-biting weeks lay ahead. I'm a fool: late in the Spring I was writing something for the *Yorkshire Post* and the features editor happened to ask me if I'd got anything else in the pipeline and I told him about the Barnsley FC job, and he told a reporter, and they printed a little bit on the front page one slow Monday about me being Barnsley's first Premiership signing, and then all hell broke loose. It started slowly and built up: Radio Ulster rang me, and I did a live interview; I wandered around on a mobile 'phone talking live to Alan Beswick on GMR. I was on Talk Radio twice in the same day and neither producer knew I'd been on the other show. I must have done thirty radio and TV interviews, and it's still carrying on. But I'm jumping the gun.

Premiership fever last Summer went hand-in-hand with Season Ticket Nerves. I didn't have a season ticket when we were in the First Division mainly because I took varying amounts of kids. I've got three of my own and I sometimes took my late brother-in-law's two. Sometimes I took one child, sometimes five. But for the Premiership we would all need season tickets, and word began to spread that they had all gone; that there were nine left; that there were thousands left; that they were going to build a new stand so that everybody could get in.

Then it was announced in the *Barnsley Chronicle* that after the existing season ticket holders had got theirs, and after the club lottery ticket holders had got theirs, then holders of ten ticket stubs from previous league games could get theirs. Ten ticket stubs: that meant sixty stubs. I'd saved all mine and the kids had saved all theirs. We made piles of them. Fifty six. We dug in pockets and behind drawers. Fifty eight. Then my wife pointed out that for ten ticket stubs you got two season tickets. So we only needed thirty. And we'd got fifty eight. We were rich!

It was a strange, mad time to be in the town; tales of huge queues at the box office were bandied around. All the season tickets would be gone before they got to the ten-stubbers. All the season tickets had gone on the first day. There were never more than two hundred season tickets available.

As I said, I always wake up before the alarm clock. I went to bed ridiculously early on the Friday night before I had to go and queue for my season tickets. I set the alarm for four thirty in the morning. I fell in and out of sleep, listening to 5 Live on my headphones. I knew that I would wake up before the alarm clock and so I switched it off. And I fell deeply asleep. And suddenly it was twenty past five, and it felt like the middle of the afternoon. I fell out of bed and got dressed.

I'll never forget that long, slow walk in the early morning mist. Three miles from my house to Oakwell. Up Tempest Avenue to the main Barnsley/Doncaster road. Along the road, past the pig farm and the curious cows. Across the valley, the hazy streetlights of Wombwell, and beyond that the darkness where Manvers coking plant used to be. Through Ardsley, past the crematorium and the student hall of residence that used to be an old people's home. There were lights on in a couple of the student rooms; they couldn't be up already, surely? Barnsley never used to have a student population, just a few mining engineers at the tech, but now the popular music course at the College was attracting people from all over the country and there were indie band nights at some of the pubs. I began to walk more quickly now, and I began to sweat. As I bent to tie my shoelaces a bus went past. Still, it wasn't far to go. I'd be quite near the front of the season ticket queue, because nobody in Barnsley got up early these days.

I turned down the hill past the monumental masons; ahead of me were the Oakwell floodlights, and my heart began to beat a bit faster, like it always did. It was ten past six in the morning.

I got to the car park and stood there, just stood there. The car park was completely full, and I could see a snake of people from the box office, right round the walls of the club. There must have been two thousand people: men, women, children. Some were drinking beer, some were cooking breakfast on small stoves. A van rolled up selling bacon sarnies and cups of tea. A car full of coppers watched warily. I made my way to the back of the queue. People I knew waved at me. A man I sometimes saw on the bus said he'd been there since ten o'clock the previous night. I stood there. An old man stood behind me, and behind him stood a man with a chair. This was it: Barnsley in the Premiership, a town that had had years and years of terrible news was now queueing up for the good news. The Holy Grail: season tickets and a chance to play Manchester United instead of Port Vale. The old man behind me spoke, with a voice like gravel: 'Me and the wife are supposed to be going to see the Endeavour at Whitby at half-past nine,' he said. 'I've come all the way from Hull,' said the man with the chair. Funny thing, but he never sat on that chair all morning.

So we stood there, not moving, talking about games. About the great game when we got promoted, April 26th, beating Bradford two-nil, goals by Paul Wilkinson and Clint Marcelle, about the time we were all walking home through the car park when we heard that Wolves had been beaten in the sixth minute of extra time by Reading, and we all danced the conga round the cars. We talked about the coming season, about how we stood quite a good chance against a lot of the teams, about how there were two premierships and we might not be able to beat Liverpool but we could certainly beat Southampton.

Time passed, slowly. News filtered back that the box office had opened. A mobile 'phone rang. It was the old man's. He took it out of his pocket. 'That'll be the Ayatollah,' he said. He held it too close to his mouth. 'Speak,' he barked. We heard his wife's voice saying that it was half past nine and they should be going to Whitby to see the Endeavour. 'I'm on my own bloody endeavour here,' he said, and we knew what he meant. The queue began to move, achingly slowly. Rumours flew and we tried to ignore them. A man three or four people behind me in the queue was counting his stubs, obsessively. 'Thirty stubs,' he said, 'for six season tickets.' 'Like me,' I said. 'I've got thirty.' 'They're mainly from the one game; I went round the seats picking 'em up sometime last winter. Good job I saved 'em.' There was a silence. The old man with the mobile 'phone spoke. 'You have to have 'em from ten different games,' he said. The subsequent swapping passed some more time.

Someone came out of the box office with a policeman. The policeman shouted. 'Will you all listen please! Will you all listen!' The person from the box office's voice was quieter, but we got the gist: there were nearly three thousand of us in the queue, but they could only process eight hundred that day. The rest of us could either go home and come back to queue tomorrow or we could put our forms and our money and our kids' birth certificates and our late brother-in-law's kids' birth certificates in a numbered envelope and we'd be dealt with in order.

'Can we have a receipt?' someone shouted.

'No, but we'll staple the envelopes up,' said the person from the box office.

So there we were, a microcosm of the history of northern life, trusting all our hopes and fears to someone with a box, watching our precious birth certificates and cash get stapled up. It was after dinner now, and I needed to go for the bus home. 'Still, at least, we're in the Premiership,' I said to the man with the chair.

'Yes,' he said, 'now the adventure can begin.' And the season stretched in front of us, holding all our dreams like you hold a precious ornament, or an ornament you've been told is precious. And I went home and waited for August.

It's a hot Summer's evening.
My wife flicks a moth out of the door
With her bra. It could have been my

Shirt, or the *Radio Times*. The sun
Has got his hat on, and the garden's
Almost dark. The hedgehog'll

Be out soon. The big wheel is going
Round, says my wife in a different place
And a different time. I'd like

To help with the moth, but I'm all
Tangled up with some fishing line
That my son left under the ironing

Board, so I'm like a swan, tangled
In the invisible knots that can choke
You or at least stop you flying.

There's a storm somewhere in the air
Which is the best place for it. It's hard
To be a moth, or a swan, or a hedgehog,

Or a big wheel. Spot them all.

Excluded

I've got this proud boast; it's a boast built carefully over years and years of standing up in public in front of all kinds of audiences in all sorts of settings from (as it says in my publicity) theatres to prisons, from front rooms to fields. My proud boast is that I can't be embarrassed. Nothing makes me go red and wish I was the size of a processed pea. A red processed pea.

And yet, here I am, head down, not catching anyone's eye, feeling an urge to put a balaclava on, change my name by deed poll and go and live in New Zealand. The far side of New Zealand. The setting for this rare moment of Ian McMillan's blazing cheeks is the Exclusion Unit in Doncaster: it's a place where 16-year-olds, who've been excluded from mainstream school for whatever reason, go for a certain number of days a week, and I'm here to bring them the Arts. You see, one of the things I do is that I'm a Community Artist. Most people, when they say that the Arts are for everybody, mean that everybody can go and look at the Arts; that they can leave their little terraced houses with the satellite dishes on the wall and the family snaps on the mantlepiece and they can go on the bus to the theatre and enjoy opera with the rest of 'em. Well, Community Artists believe that everybody can make Art of every sort, not just look at it or listen to it, and that the Arts should be inclusive, not exclusive.

So that's why I'm here, at the Exclusion Unit. I'm including the excluded in Art. Except at this point in the space/time continuum they don't seem to want it. I'm here with a visual artist and a musician and we're introducing everybody to everybody else with a naming rap: 'Well I walked down Beckett Road today, and I saw some people coming my way . . .' and so on. And it usually works. It's often a great ice-breaker and it begins to include the excluded. Usually. Not today. I feel like a curate turning up at a youth club with a ping pong bat and a New Kids on the Block album. I feel daft. I feel that the Excluded are excluding me. They're sitting there in curlicues of embarrassment, pulling hats down lower over their faces, sinking into their coats, not looking at us, looking with deep concentration at the floor. As we gamely struggle on with the naming rap they do an extraordinary thing:

44

they pull their coats over their faces like pantomime villains or black-and-white Draculas, and it's a defining moment for me, and maybe for them.

When the first caveman or cavewoman drew the first line on a cave wall I'm sure there wasn't that division between artist and non-artist. When one cave person put the painting stick down then another cave person picked the painting stick up, and maybe that's how the relay was invented, too. And then like a slide show of evolution the cave people stood up erect and their sticks became brushes and they became cartoon images of artists with berets and palettes and easels, lifting reflective thumbs up to impassive nudes, and somewhere along the route of that slide show, that cartoon, art stopped being inclusive and became exclusive.

And I'm worried. Oh, it ended up okay in the Exclusion Unit, and we made some good artwork and some fine music and wrote some splendid poems and eventually they looked at us and talked to us and maybe liked us a but and maybe, more importantly, began to see themselves as artists, but the Exclusion Unit's just a gravy stain on the shirt of life. You can tell I'm a poet. I was reading a newspaper survey recently: they'd asked lots of people what the lottery board should spend its good cause money on. These were people on the street. Smiling people, people with houses and ties, people who read books and maybe people who listen to Radio 4. And none of them said that lottery money should be spent on the Arts. They trundled out the old sacred cows: spend it on sick children, on housing, on removing dog dirt, on public transport. And when I read that I feel myself going red again; I'm red with anger this time, not embarrassment: I think that there's no point in having a house and a job and a clean street if you're excluded. Excluded from the process of Art. Without taking part in Art we're just battery chickens who some-times go on foreign holidays. And that's why I'm in places like the Exclusion Unit doing a naming rap. Well, that and the glory. See you at the mural workshop.

The Long Dark Corridor of Winter

A poem in the style of George Formby

It's dark!
It's long!
It's the long dark corridor of winter!

It's long!
It's dark!
It's the dark long corridor of winter!

After Christmas, all you get
is freezing cold and soaking wet;
my Lancashire hot pot turns to ice
and missis, that's not very nice.

Three months of underheated gloom
like laying out a corpse in a cold front room
tell me just me what I can do
when me ukelele's turning blue!

It's dark!
It's long!
It's the long dark corridor of winter!

It's long!
It's dark!
It's the dark long corridor of winter!

I'm from Lancashire not Finland
but I feel like an arctic bloke
when you have to thaw your breath out to see what you're saying
It really is no joke!

Dark in the morning, dark at night
ghostly mills in ghostly light
I'm not feeling very bright
when winter grips me pencil tight!

It's dark
It's long
It's the long dark corridor of winter

It's long!
It's dark!
It's the dark long corridor of winter!

In the Picture

Last week I was waiting at a bus stop for the Doncaster bus when a car screeched up and bounced to a halt. A couple on the front seat were arguing furiously and I tried to listen whilst pretending to study the vapour trails of aeroplanes coming down to or taking off from Leeds Bradford airport. After quite a lot of shouting the woman jumped from the car and slammed the door, for a time much less than a tenth of a second she glanced at me and then ran off up the road. The man glanced at me for a time much less than a fifth of a second and then drove off down the road. And the point is that somehow, in some vague flickering image at the edge of their eyes, I figure in that couple's memory. Or memories, if that incident at the bus stop was the last straw and they split up before the Paris shuttle had landed on Runway three. Maybe, in years to come, they'll meet in a wine bar in somewhere unlikely and they'll laugh and say 'Remember that fat bloke in the red shirt who was at the bus stop when we had that daft row and we ran off and drove off', and there I'll be, the spectre at the feast, the unknown cousin at the wedding, the signature on the Christmas card that you just can't make out.

It's a kind of immortality, really, this being at the edge of the picture. It means that you nag and nag at the corner of somebody's mind because they can only half remember you and by being there you somehow bring the bigger memories into sharper focus. Where was it that I saw the fat bloke: Tenby, looking longingly at a pork pie. That's right. Tenby, and that was a really nice holiday . . .

But what if you could take it a tiny stage further and actually try and force yourself into people's memories by doing something silly? I could go to, say, Trafalgar Square wearing a hat that lit up in neon lights with the word 'Madagascar' on it, and loads of people would see me and laugh and then a couple of months later a couple on a first date would be nervously chatting and one of them would say, 'I saw a really funny thing in Trafalgar Square this Summer: I saw a bloke in a big hat with "Madagascar" on it,' and the other one would say, 'Yes, you won't believe this but I was there too, and I saw him and didn't he look daft . . .' and love begins to blossom, thanks to you and the daft hat. And the memory could cross generations: my dad tells the tale of a man from his home village in Scotland in the Thirties who took a trip by train to Edinburgh and got off the train, looked round the station and then went back home. 'What's Edinburgh like?' his mates asked him. 'It's full of steam and covered in glass,' the man said, and my dad told it to me and now I'm telling it to you and there's that man in Waverley station looking round at the ceiling and imprinted in all our memories like a watermark.

I think it should be your resolution, your *carpe diem*, to try and graft yourself into the edge of at least one person's memory each day. Shout a silly word on the bus. Drop a tomato on the shoe shop floor. Hold up a photograph of a hen on the ferry. Play a trumpet in a museum. You'll become a kind of social glue. People will remember the day by you. You'll be a talisman, an emblem. Some couples have their song, but even more couples have their shared memory. Carry a balloon and a frog down the main street of any town and I guarantee that you'll never die. You'll live on like pre-decimal currency and a folk-memory of a time when everyone smoked and wore a hat. What more could you ask?

Endless Shedness

lift lid of shed peer into
endless shedness below

a kind of blue sky shedness
a kind of endless shedness
like the corners you find in sheds

like your shed has more corners
than you thought possible

endless shedness
you always find things in your shed
that you never put there
that your parents never put there
that your children never put there
endless shedness

try this now
with your own shed
and you will find the
(endless shedness)
things that were never put there

endless shedness
endless shed
e   ess s   ess
e   e   e   e
   less shed
   less hed
endless shed
endless shed

Fear of Falling

It's time to face the fear. It's time to look the fear in the eye and spit. In a minute. In a minute I'll face the fear and I'll spit. That's how I thought it would be: I thought I could repeat some kind of mantra and I'd be okay. I've just come back from two weeks in Mexico, reading my poems to baffled Mexicans and making a TV travel programme, and I had to face a lot of fear. I had to spit a lot. I had to learn a great deal about myself.

Flying. Grasshoppers. Horses. Three words: lots of spit. Flying was the first fear. The last time I'd flown was a holiday hop down to Guernsey last summer, and I'd held on to the sides of the seat and left my seatbelt fastened all the way. I was like The Condemned Man. My kids were saying things like 'Hey Dad, look at the way the houses are all on a slant when you first take off,' and 'Hey Dad look, we're way above the clouds.' I was saying things like 'Shut Up' and 'I'll be okay.' And now I had an eleven-hour flight from Gatwick to Mexico City, and then over the two-week jaunt I had six internal flights. So I was terrified for eleven hours. I kept my eyes shut. I didn't see any of the three films. I didn't eat either of the meals. We landed and I held on tight. 'That wasn't so bad, was it?' said the TV producer who was travelling with me. I couldn't reply because my jaws were jammed shut. His next words made me go cold and hot at the same time. 'We'll be doing a bit of filming on the plane to Oaxaca tomorrow,' he said, 'just a short piece to camera.' A piece to camera. That meant I had to have my eyes open and it wouldn't be very good if I was dribbling. That night in my hotel room I looked at myself in the mirror and said 'It's Time to Face the Fear. It's Time to Face the Fear and Spit.' I spat at the mirror. It didn't make a lot of difference. I was still terrified.

But the next day I climbed on the plane and somehow I conquered the fear. My mirror was covered in spit and my voice was shaking to start with but eventually I did the piece to camera and after a while I dared to look out of the window and look at the tiny houses below, and as we landed I dared to admit to myself that I was enjoying it. And I felt good. And that night in the bar the producer said to me, 'Tomorrow you're going to eat grasshoppers,'

51

and I swallowed my beer quickly and had another one. Late into the night my mirror stared back at me damply. In bed I contemplated the random nature of fear. Maybe a fear of flying is justified; you're high in the air in a metal tube, but a fear of eating grasshoppers?

The next day they faced me on the plate. The lights were on and the camera focused in the tiny Mexican restaurant in an Oaxacan suburb. They didn't really look like grasshoppers, which helped a bit. They looked like small pieces of abandoned raffia. 'Stick your fork in and get a good mouthful,' said the producer gleefully. There was a roaring in my ears. My whole life was leading up to this moment. The waiter was called Omar and he was smiling. A fly landed on my hand. I concentrated hard on not vomiting. I plunged the fork in. I ate a few. The producer made me do it again. 'Make vigorous chewing movements,' he said. 'It looks good on camera.' I plotted his painful death. I ate them, and they weren't too bad. It was like eating tiny toothpicks.

Now I began to feel good. I was Facing the Fear. Flying, Pah! Pass me my goggles! Grasshoppers? I'll have 'em on toast. 'Good,' said the producer, 'tomorrow you ride the horse.'

And that is where it all failed, it all fell to tiny pieces. The random nature of fear: flying conquered, grasshoppers munched, horses looming like huge great horse balloons floating across the sky of my bedroom. I always walk on the other side of the road even when the horse is tied up in a field. I shy away from the peaceful ones they have at football matches. As a kid I never even rode donkeys on the beach. We went to a cowboy ranch and the cowboys rode up and down lassooing things. The horses looked athletic and powerful and scary. I said to the producer, 'I really don't think I can do this,' and he said, 'I'll help you up.' I said, 'I do most things for you, but I honestly, and I'm being quite serious here, I honestly don't believe I can get on a horse.' I felt like I was going to cry. He said, 'I'll get one of the cowboys to help you up.' And I wish I could say that it was marvellous. I sat there. The horse moved. I wanted to die. I smiled at the camera like a death mask of Coco the Clown. My voice wavered like Miss Marple's.

The random nature of fear. Some you win: grasshoppers, flying. Some you lose: horses. I can't understand fear and I don't want to. It's good to be frightened of some things; it keeps a perspective on the world. It gives you light and shade, gives you a sort of slide rule to judge things by. Was it frightening? Well, it was the horse side of a single-engined plane. Good job nobody mentioned slugs while we were in Mexico. The air would have been heavy with spit then. Really heavy with spit.

Little Billy Jones and his Nasty Mother

Little Billy Jones
had a box of Rhino Bones

He kept them hidden
underneath his bed.

Mrs Lily Jones
hated Billy's Rhino Bones

so she chucked them in the river
then she said

   'I'm sorry, Billy,
   Been so silly
   You'll never guess what I've done!

   I've committed a sin
   Put your bones in the bin
   Now they're on the tip, my son!'

Little Billy Jones
loved his box of Rhino Bones,

he wept and wailed
and wailed and blubbed and wept.

Mrs Lily Jones
forgot Billy's Rhino Bones

and the story would have ended there
except . . .

    Listen to the pounding of the Rhino Feet
    Up the Jones's suburban street
    Listen to the sound of the Rhino Roar
    Up the Jones's path, at the Jones Front Door

See Lily Jones
Quite forlorn
Impaled on a great sharp
Rhino Horn

See Lily Jones
Somehow aloof
Squashed beneath a two ton
Rhino Hoof.

Lily Jones was Billy's Mother
Now she's flatter than a knife
She didn't know that when you add water to Rhino Bones
It brings the rhino to life

Ho ho

It brings the rhino to life!

MORAL:

If you chuck bones in the river
make sure that they're your own.

McMillan's Symphony of Light

It started in a small way, as all the great spiritual and artistic quests do. Often, on a Winter's morning, I have to walk down our road to the bus stop to get the early bus. It's dark, and it's cold, and there's only me on the street, unless I see The Man with the Dog and the Torch. He walks his dog on the fields at the back of our road, and he has a torch to light his way, and it's somehow comforting. Sometimes I see the Cheerful Milkman, and his milk-float is lit up like Blackpool Illuminations on our dark street. Sometimes I see them both on the same day, and maybe the first time I saw them both on the same day was the start of my quest.

Or maybe it was the day I saw both the aeroplanes. Aircraft pass over our village on the way to Leeds/Bradford airport and when I'm walking down for the bus I often see one going across the sky from right to left with its lights winking, and I sometimes see one going across the sky from left to right with its lights wink-ing. Once, I saw them both, lights winking in the early morning and perhaps that's where the quest was born.

I decided that I wouldn't be satisfied, in an artistic and spiri-tual way, until all four things happened at once, on the same day: the Man with the Dog and the Torch, the Cheerful Milkman, and the two planes crossing in the sky. Conditions had to be right: it had to be a clear dark morning. There had to be no clouds, and there had to be a touch of frost. I called my quest McMillan's Symphony of Light, and I never told anybody else about it until now, although I did briefly consider applying to the Arts Council for a grant for it as a piece of conceptual art.

The trouble was, the symphony began to grow. After a spate of burglaries in the area, lots of houses in the street got security lights, the kind that are activated when someone walks past them. I found that I could play the street like some kind of Light Piano, lighting up number 9, number 13, number 27 and num-ber 31. Somebody moved into number 32, and occasionally, as I walked past, their bathroom light would be switched on. Now it was getting difficult and Mahleresque, my Symphony of Light. The two planes had to cross in the sky. I had to see The Man with the Dog and the Torch and the Cheerful Milkman. I had to switch

56

on all the security lights as I went by, and the bathroom light had to come on at just the right time. It was like waiting for an eclipse, or a rare comet, or East Fife four Forfar five on the Scottish football results.

Sometimes, tantalisingly, it would almost work, but the Cheerful Milkman would be late or the security light at number 27 would be broken or it would be cloudy and I couldn't see the planes. Sometimes I wouldn't have to catch the early bus but I couldn't enjoy my lie in because I'd be thinking – perhaps this would have been the day.

And of course, over the years, as the 'nineties progressed into the late 'nineties, the quest got slightly more complex and subtle. It had to be frosty, because a security light shining on frost is beautiful. I had to see the cat whose eyes were reflected in the Cheerful Milkman's headlights. The postwoman had to come by with her reflective jacket on. Sometimes, late at night, I'd consider engineering it, just to get the quest over and done with. I'd slip the Cheerful Milkman a fiver just to turn the corner at a certain time and I'd ask the bloke at number 32 to turn his bathroom light on at a given signal. But of course it wouldn't work because the thing had to be driven by chance and coincidence, like life is, and anyway, on the day that I directed it like Cecil B. DeMille the cat wouldn't turn up because you can never rely on cats.

I'd love to report, for this last *Fourth Column* of the series, that it actually happened the other day: the Man with the Torch and the Dog, the Cheerful Milkman, the security lights and the frost, the aeroplanes in the clear sky, the bathroom light, the reflective postwoman, the cat's glinting eyes, but it didn't, and it hasn't, and it probably never will.

It nearly did last week, but it wasn't frosty. I came close on a freezing February morning in 1996 but the postwoman was on holiday. It could have all come together in late November 1996 but it was foggy. Never mind. It's better to travel hopefully than arrive, as the man said, or maybe it's better to travel wonderingly to a bus stop on a chilly morning in the knackered North of England than to walk around all your life with your eyes shut, as the man should have said.

Cautionary Playground Rhyme

Natasha Green
Natasha Green
stuck her head in a washing machine

Washing Machine
Washing Machine
round and round Natasha Green

Natasha Green
Natasha Green
cleanest girl I've ever seen

Ever Seen
Ever Seen
a girl with her head in a washing machine?

Washing Machine
Washing Machine
last home of Natasha Green

Natasha Green
Natasha Green
washed away in a white machine

White Machine
White Machine
soaped to death Natasha Green

Natasha Green
Natasha Green
cleanest ghost I've ever seen!

MORAL:

Washing machines are for knickers and blouses
Washing machines are for jumpers and trousers
Keep your head out of the washing machine
or you'll end up as spotless as little Miss Green.

You Always Hurt the One You Love

I popped into our local art gallery the other day, to get out of the rain. I took my cagoule off and hung it on the coatstand, and stood in front of a huge picture of Sir John Harvey Jones. After a while I stood in front of a huge picture of Sir John Mills and then I stood in front of a huge picture of Sir Yehudi Menuhin. The curator, Don, was having his morning cup of coffee by the retail outlet and I went to have a word with him before I ventured back out into the Barnsley rain. Don was flicking through a magazine for people who worked in Art Galleries and Museums and I don't remember the name of it but it was probably called something sexy like *Art Galleries and Museums Monthly*. Don looked at me, looked at my cagoule, and passed me the magazine. I glanced at the piece and time stood still. I felt an awful thundering sense of guilt. I felt like I'd been found out. I felt like my cagoule was a lethal weapon. Yehudi Menuhin's eyes burned into me and I turned away in shame.

The thrust of the article was that visitors to galleries and museums give off a kind of miasma or hum or ectoplasm, particularly if they come in out of the rain, and this mist is destroying the art and artefacts they're gazing at. It's a proven fact that most people go to galleries to escape the weather, and by the very act of walking through the doors they're making civilisation crumble, at the very least. I didn't know where to look. I felt that I was endangering Don's livelihood just by being there. The steam from Don's coffee wafted into the air, bringing the return of the Dark Ages a little closer as it did so. I love art galleries and museums. I feel that I'm growing slightly as a human being every time I go into one. Well, until now, that is. Until the revelation that my wetness, my condensation, was helping the art to fade away. Don took the magazine off me and silently turned the page. He pointed to another paragraph, and I clenched my buttocks in shame and went bright red.

Not only do visitors to galleries and museums create their own personal cloud of wet rot, they also fart a great deal and these emissions are causing even more damage to our culture. It's the methane, apparently. I felt slightly dizzy as I recalled the little peep I'd squeezed out by Sir John Harvey Jones. I didn't dare move. I stood rooted, as they say in novels, to the spot.

I'm annihilating art just by going to the gallery. My sweaty thumbs are flaking my library books away. My heavy boots are churning up the paths I love to walk on. The precious silence of the world is cracked asunder by these words on the radio. Each time I hold my children's hands I'm wearing their skin away, turning it into household dust. Whenever I kiss my wife minute particles of her lips are lost.

And the worst bit is that my trumps are turning Sir John Harvey Jones into a shadow of his former self.

I picked up my cagoule, carefully, so as not to disturb any of the molecules in the air, and left the gallery. Outside it was still raining, and the rain was eating into the Town Hall and the Barnsley Building Society. A bus went by, through a puddle, splashing my legs, and my trousers were that much closer to the jumble sale. I got on the bus and my ticket was destroying forests, and the exhausts of all the vehicles were turning the air into that kind of stuff you find in the plughole when you haven't washed the sink for a while. When I got home, I just sat there, very still, my buttocks barely touching the settee. I turned the pages of a magazine very carefully, wiping my hands after each turn. My wife was watching TV. 'That Yehudi Menuhin's aged a lot recently,' she said, gesturing at the screen. Not as much as me, my love; not as much as me.

Longbow Bonfire Farewell

[The Longbow Pub's community bonfire in my village has ended after twenty glorious years, so there won't be one tonight]

No Flowers in the sky over the pig farm.
No Pigs saying the flowers in the sky are blooming.
No Committee men nipping to the Longbow.
No Flowers in the sky over Uncle Donald's house.
No Committee men holding raffle tickets too tightly.
No Pigs saying look at the sky.
No Children parading their guys for inspection.
No Committee man sitting in a pram being a guy.
No Bored pilot flying overhead from Leeds/Bradford Airport.
No Worms deep below the bonfire looking up.
No Crying woman shouting Malcolm.
No Carnations in the sky over the pig farm.
No Children of mine clutching candy floss.
No Glimpse of Uncle Donald's tache in the firelight.
No Fat bloke in a Crewe Alexandra shirt.
No Committee men holding pints too tightly.
No Community policeman remaining impassive.
No Elderly people in the home asking for the TV to be turned
    up.
No Children of mine looking at roses in the sky.
No Worms deep below the bonfire burrowing deeper.
No Incongruous Santa with a queue of children.
No Flames bursting higher than the ones you remember.
No Pigs saying I don't like the darkness between the bursting
    flowers.
No See you next year at the Longbow bonfire.
No Snogging behind the committee shed.
No Guys sitting there like plastic bags with masks.
No Committee men standing with crushed plastic glasses.
No Knowledge that the fire will die.
No Pigs saying it seems to have been a long time since the last
    burning flower.
No Single mask frowning from the grass.

No Incongruous Santa taking his beard off in the Longbow
     .toilets.
No Pigs saying I think the burning flowers have ended for this
     year.
Nothing to light the long darkness.
Nothing to light the long darkness.

I once read about this man in New York who was walking down the street, minding his own business, thinking about nothing, butterflies flapping around inside his head, when he saw a playing card on the floor. He picked it up: a three of hearts, wilting in the New York heat, and in that moment he stopped thinking about nothing and the butterflies stopped flapping around inside his head. They were replaced by playing cards, cascading like confetti. Now the man's days had a glittering purpose; he spent the rest of his life, head down, wandering the streets of New York looking for enough playing cards to make a full set. Sometimes he went for months without finding one; sometimes he went for months without finding one, and then when he found one it was one he'd already got. Another Jack of Spades!

That man, and his pointless quest, has haunted me for years. When I was a teenager I resolved to do the same thing after two pints of bitter at The Bridge Inn. I searched for weeks around the streets of Barnsley, fruitlessly. Then I found one! At last, my quest had begun. I turned it over: Master Bun, the baker's son. Well, Barnsley's never been New York.

Somehow, when you find things on the street, even pointless things that you don't want, the actual finding of them conveys a kind of mystical status that they wouldn't have if they were lying round in your house. A seven of clubs on the coffee table doesn't give any kind of existential *coup de foudre*, but a seven of clubs on 42nd Street does.

Then I went to an exhibition of shoes at an art gallery in Hull; the artist's daughter had run away a lot when she was in her teens, and he'd spent a lot of time walking round cities looking for her, and although he usually found her, what he also found was a lot of shoes, single shoes, or pumps, or wellies, or, in one case, a flipper. And the amazing thing was that they looked so sad (in the old, rather than the new sense of the word) on their own in the gallery; they were mystical, like the playing cards, but they were also heartbreaking. It's true that you don't often hear the word 'heartbreaking' applied to a flipper, but take my word for it.

So the playing cards and the shoes set me off; I'd make my

own collection of profound *objets trouvés*, and I knew exactly what I would be going for: The Single Industrial Glove.

You must have noticed them, often in the middle of the road, sometimes waving, sometimes pointing, sometimes making obscene gestures with one or more fingers. Sometimes they're new ones, dropped by accident from the lorry of an optimistic small builder who's done his own signwriting on the side of an ancient Bedford van. Sometimes they're ancient, fingers gone, thumbs ragged, after months and months gripping the shovel or the trowel. I spent a day looking for them and I came across three: two red ones and a blue one. I took them home in a carrier bag marked FRESH TODAY. I put them on the table. I looked at them, three gloves lying there like long dead fish. They didn't look profound. They didn't deliver any kind of existential *coup de* anything. They look daft. My wife came in. 'Why have you bought three gloves?' she said. I tried to explain about found objects and the way they achieved a kind of higher significance when you put them somewhere incongruous, like the table, but even as I said it I began to falter. The gloves just sat there, the fingers inert.

My wife went into the other room to get her library books. I chucked the industrial gloves in the bin, and I thought that was it for finding things, until I was on the top deck of the bus and I noticed the glittery strips in the hedge. Now you must have seen these; bits of discarded cassette tape, thrown out of the windows of cars by disgruntled reps, and somehow caught in the bushes. Now that would be a thing to collect; something even more fundamentally sorrowful than single industrial glove . . . lost music, flapping in the breeze. So I got off the bus at the next stop and pulled a bit of tape off, about a foot and a half. I could stick 'em in an album. I could stick a number together and play them, although it would probably come out as Johnny Mathis.

That was yesterday. I've already filled two pages in my album. Want to see it? I call it The Human Condition. It's amazing what you find when you look, or rather it's amazing what you find inside the things you find. Now that's profound. I think I'll tape it and then chuck it in a hedge.

The Twelve Surrealist Days of Christmas

on the first day of christmas my surrealist true love gave to me
a partridge in a pair of pin striped trousers

on the second day of christmas my surrealist true love gave to me
two glass euphoniums
and a partridge in a pair of pin striped trousers

on the third day of christmas my surrealist truc love gave to me
three french wasps
two glass euphoniums
and a partridge in a pair of pin striped trousers

on the fourth day of christmas my surrealist truc love gave to me
four barbed wire breasts
three french wasps
two glass euphoniums
and a partridge in a pair of pin striped trousers

on the fifth day of christmas my surrealist true love gave to me
five gold giraffes
four barbed wire breasts
three french wasps
two glass euphoniums
and a partridge in a pair of pin striped trousers

on the sixth day of christmas my surrealist true love gave to me
six geese a-playing huge flutes made of cheese

on the seventh day of christmas my surrealist true love gave to me
seven swansea a to z's with the letter f's cut out

on the eighth day of christmas my surrealist true love gave to me
eight cardboard hovercrafts

on the ninth day of christmas my surrealist true love gave to me
nothing because nine isn't a surrealist number

on the tenth day of christmas my surrealist true love gave to me
glob dib dob nib nob

on the eleventh day of christmas my surrealist true love gave to me
eleven full size lego models of lego models of elvis

on the twelfth day of christmas my true love gave to me
twelve bottled hedgehog farts

Minimalism

I like minimalism. I like the kind of art that's a few specks in the corner of the canvas and I like the kind of music that's a few scratchings at the corner of the ear. I like things that offer very slight variations on each other, like a row of bean cans in the supermarket, or a pile of shirts in a shirt shop. And that's why I love our Autumn day out in Cleethorpes. The same things always happen; nothing changes. Our Autumn day out is a still point in a changing world.

Actually, the same things start to happen the night before, when I pop across the road to my mother's to tell her we're going and she dips into her purse and gives me some money for the kids. I smile, knowing that the ball is starting to roll, and that the same things will happen, beautifully, gorgeously.

The next morning the kids argue, like they always do, about who will sit in the middle. None of them wants to: one of them will have to. It's some kind of Life Lesson. Then my wife checks the tyre pressure. It's only a seventy mile run, but she checks the tyre pressure. My wife gets in the car and, like she always does, gives me that look that says 'I wish you could drive'. Lovely. She's been giving me that look for twenty years.

Then we're off: we drive past my mother, waving from the upstairs window like she always does when we go on our Autumn Day Out to Cleethorpes. The kids argue: radio or tapes. We go the same route, towards Doncaster, down the A1, down the M18, onto the M180, always the same route. We're like a little mini-malist exhibition, all on our own. We see the same things: the sewerage works that looks like some kind of lottery-funded bus station, the hedge where we once saw three dead badgers in a row, the place where we once saw a tiny deer running up a garden path past a woman hanging washing out. The sun always goes in as we approach the east coast and it's wonderfully familiar, excellently the same.

We approach Grimsby, passing a sign that says Great Grimsby, Europe's Food Town, and I always say, in a mock Dr Watson voice, 'Great Grimsby, Holmes, how do you do it?' and the kids make small noises signifying disgust and stare out at the fish

67

finger factory. Then it's Guess the Temperature on the Grimsby *Evening Telegraph* Building, a marvellous game for all the family, then it's Look at Grimsby's Football Ground, then it's Is the Tide In or Out? Then it's Can You See The Donkeys? Then it's Is The Little Train Running?

All the familiar things pile up, like little comforters, little smiley faces in an otherwise hostile universe.

Then we drive through Cleethorpes to Humberston, for the real purpose of our Autumn Day Out, which is to see my wife's parents in the caravan they've been in since May; they'll only be here for another week or so, and then they'll admit that Summer's really over and come back to Barnsley to winter like migrating birds. The delicious sameness will continue. My mother-in-law will make the best Yorkshire puddings you've ever seen, my father-in-law will cut generous slices of lamb from a far-too-big joint, the kids will go to the running-down camp shop and buy daft things like pencil drawings of Blur or Skeleton Money Boxes, and then we'll go for a walk and my mother-in-law will say, 'I think we'll come home next week. It's getting a bit cold at night', and then we'll all be happy, and the kids will know that, as it always does at this time of year, the slippery slope to Christmas has begun.

Philip Bleachdrinker

Philip Bleachdrinker
drank a lot of bleach
so his daddy put the bleach
on a high shelf out of reach.

Mr Bleachdrinker
was used to Philip's ways,
how he glugged down bleach for days
with a speed that would amaze.

Philip Bleachdrinker
was a cunning little man.
He hatched a clever plan
to smack his daddy with a pan.

Mr Bleachdrinker
took the pan right in the gob
gave a stifled sniffy sob
and called his son a yob.

Philip Bleachdrinker
in the very best of health
climbed up to the shelf
and began to help himself . . .

Then

Philip Bleachdrinker
felt the shelf begin to tip
felt himself begin to slip
fell down onto his lip.

Mr Bleachdrinker
saw the bottle hit his son
saw the damage done
saw the tears begin to run.

Philip Bleachdrinker
felt the bottle strike his skull
with a sound both loud and dull
the bottle was really full.

Mr Bleachdrinker
saw his son begin to weep
as he lay there in a heap
and he wished he was asleep.

MORAL

Just because you're called Bleachdrinker
doesn't mean you must drink bleach,
my mate Mr Frank Sandchewer
doesn't spend his time eating the beach!

I hadn't seen Frank for months. I normally bumped into him late at night walking his dog by the old pit ponds. When the moon was full, it often gleamed on his pate, but I never laughed. Not until I got home, anyway. Then I laughed until I cried, and the neighbours banged on the wall with a brush. That's life in South Yorkshire these days, laughing or crying, walking a dog or banging on the wall with a brush.

Anyway, the other night I was in the bus shelter waiting for the last 212 when Frank walked past. He didn't have his dog, and he had his hood up, so I didn't recognise him at first, but I knew that nobody else in Barnsley shuffled like that, so I said 'Frank?' and he jumped up like he'd been shot. He looked at me with wild staring eyes, and his face looked like a wall on which somebody had banged a brush once too often. 'What have you been doing with yourself?' I asked, and he leaned closer, his breath like a representation of the Battle of the Somme in breath form. He began to speak, and his voice was low and troubled:

'You know how I got made redundant, well we all did, you know that, well you know what that leads to, don't you, walking the dog for hours, watching the telly for hours, making endless cups of tea while you build up enough energy to go down to the allotment to check on your runner beans. And then a man asks you, a man in a pub asks you, if you fancy doing a little job for him, breaking up a bit of scrap, buckshee, cash on the palm, and of course you say "yes", and you do it, and times are hard so you carry on signing on, and they've got the inspectors out, and one day they come and catch you at the scrapyard and your dole's stopped and . . .' He looked around as though somebody might be listening. 'Can you keep a secret?' he said. I nodded. 'Come wi' me,' he said, as the thunder cracked and lightning lit up the sky. I was worried about him. He looked deeply unhappy; not just the unhappy that most men look around here, but more monochrome, more crumpled. Monochrome with knobs on. Cheap knobs that most people would throw away.

We got to his allotment, walked past his runner beans to the pigeon shed; the storm was reaching its height, and I saw the last

212 making its way down the road like a reminder of good times. 'This had better be good,' I muttered to myself. Frank stood by the door of the shed. He hesitated and looked me straight in the eye through ancient glasses spattered with rain. 'What you are about to see you must never reveal to anybody,' he said. I nodded.

He opened the door to the shed. It creaked. In the middle of the shed was a huge table and there was something on it, covered over with a blanket. From under the blanket a number of metal coat hangers protruded, attached to an electric lawn mower and an old toaster. The thunder was deafening now, so Frank had to shout to make himself heard. 'This is the solution to all the snoopers and the ones who try and catch you out!' he yelled. 'This is the answer! I've been watching them old Frankenstein films and I thought, "That doesn't look so hard. I could have a go at that." And that's what I did. I made a bloke. A bloke like me. A bloke in my own image who can go and sign on. And tonight, with the storm and the mower and the toaster, I'm going to make him live!' He fixed me with his unsettling gaze. 'It's a good toaster,' he said. 'It's from the catalogue.

Then he twiddled with the wires and pressed a button on the toaster; a flash of lightning seemed to engulf the whole shed and the lawnmower glowed red hot. Frank was laughing fit to bust and the room was filling with smoke. Frank gestured to the table. 'It's alive!' he shrieked, and the blanket fell away. Somebody who looked a bit like Frank with a faint hint of Frank's dog was lying on the table. It could have been a distant cousin of Frank, or an old photograph of Frank super-imposed over an older photograph of his dog. It had a bolt through its neck and stitches at its wrists. Bits of the person on the table looked remarkably like bits of Frank's recently departed Uncle Norman. The person on the table sat up. 'I could murder a pork pie,' he said in a high, creaking voice.

Things will never be the same at the DSS again.

Poem is a City

Poem is a city. Dark corners.
You sleep under blankets
in a poem. In the shop doorway,

in the underpass of a poem.
It is as though you cannot live
anywhere else except in a poem

is a city. Under blankets. Dark
blankets. From a moving train
you see into the houses,

the landscape is a windowscape,
a kitchenscape. 'Ah,' you say,
poetically, 'what a delightful

kettlescape in that kitchen'
because poem is a city, city
is a poem. Underpass of a poem.

Being There

I caught the bus to Doncaster the other Sunday, and because it was Sunday, it wasn't the usual driver; it was a small woman with glasses, and not the big bloke with a lot of rings. 'I'm glad I've got a passenger,' she said, 'because I don't know the route.' And that's how I became a bus driver for the day. Well, almost. I sat next to her and guided her round the estates and along the bypass. I told her when to turn right by the Rising Sun and left at the Butchers Arms. Even though I can't drive, and I've only had a couple of disastrous lessons, and I wouldn't know one end of a gearstick from another, I became a bus driver that cool Sunday, simply by being there.

I live most of my life in a state of Being There, and by Being There I think I'm Doing It. But I'm not Doing It, I'm Being There. It sounds complex, but it isn't. Taping an obscure Polish film on BBC2 and then watching it later is Doing It. Taping it and never watching it is Being There. Buying a seed catalogue is Being There. Buying a seed catalogue and planting the seeds is Doing It. Saturday nights I sit down to watch *Match of the Day*; I have a glass of wine and maybe a lump or two of cheese. As the teams run like hell up and down the pitch and punch the air when they score and threaten careers with crunching tackles, I glug my wine and munch my cheese and think that somehow, in some strange photosynthetic way, I'm getting fitter. When I actually go to the match and see the tackles and the running and the punching the air from close quarters I think I'm getting fitter still. By watching these sportsmen my belly is getting less flabby. I'm Being There when perhaps I should be Doing It.

I often walk through Barnsley and look in at the window of the music shop and read all the adverts for the gigs around town; The Brown Bottle Blues Band are on at the Plough, the Codhead Quartet are appearing at the Students Union; there's an Indie band night every Wednesday at the Ticket Office. And by reading that notice, simply by reading that notice, I think I've been to all those sweaty nights of rock and roll. But I haven't Done It, I've simply Been There, and that's not the same thing at all.

I graze Tourist Information Offices, which are Cathedrals of

Doing It, with their rows of leaflets and walls of posters. I turn them into temples of Being There, though, because I pick up dozens of leaflets for everything from military museums to ghost walks through York and I put them all behind the clock. And I've Been There, even though I haven't Done That.

And I don't know where it will end, because Doing It takes so much more effort than Being There; it would take me years and years to master Italian perfectly, but I can glance at a magazine advert for language tapes and I've Been There. Lassoing a cow on a ranch is a huge feat of Doing It, but if you watch a couple of Saturday afternoon matinees you've Been There.

And lately I'm finding that I'm Being There more and more, and Doing It less and less. I flick through a guidebook to Morocco and I'm a world traveller; I subscribe to a history magazine and even though I never read it I'm a historian. I pick up a book catalogue and even though I never buy any of the books I feel like I've read them all when I've only glanced at the titles. They used to say that people read the reviews of books rather than reading the books themselves; well, I go one further than that; I put the book review sections of news-papers in my briefcase, intending to read them on the bus, and simply by that intention I brim with cultural currency.

Help, I don't know what to do. I've been asked to write a column for the radio, but I imagine that just by receiving the invitation to write the column, I've written it and it's already been broadcast. I'm not even thinking about it and it's been written and broadcast and heard and forgotten about and even now its waves are flying by Pluto.

I'm a Human Being and I should be a Human Doing. Mind you, I can drive a bus and I'm as fit as any of the blokes on that pitch. More cheese?

Cautionary Mystery

That feller
in the yeller cap
who sits with a blanket
on his lap,

what happened to him?
What happened?

That poor old man
in the yeller hat
with a face like a cap
that's missed its flap

what happened to him, mum
what happened to him?

You don't want to know, kid
you don't want to know
it's so terrible
you don't want to know.

But that man just sits there
on his own
with a face like a sock
and a heart like a stone,

you don't want to know, son
you don't want to know.

But the man just sits there
deep in thought
with a face like a battle
that's just been fought
and hands that shake
like leaves in a breeze
and a face like rubble
and eyes like cheese . . .

You don't want to know, son
you don't want to know.

MORAL

Some things are better left unsaid
with eyes like butter and a face like bread.

Laying Blame

I blame the crisp Canadian. I blame the dark night. I blame the old straw. Oh, all right then: I blame myself. Picture the scene; the sorrowing family by the shallow grave, the clouds low and monochrome, the snow threatening somewhere in the air like the touch of a damp tea towel on the face.

I'm blinded by grief. Let me start at the beginning. I'm in a wine club and I get wine through the post. It makes me feel like I've arrived at some central fulcrum of adulthood when the man in the blue van knocks at the door and struggles in with a big clinking box. I'm here. I'm a writer and I have wine delivered to the door. This month the offer in the club catalogue was Canadian wine. Now that would be good for the man in the blue van to bring: Canadian wine! I'd be the only person on our street drinking Canadian wine!

So the Canadian wine came, the man in the blue van remaining unimpressed as he asked me to sign, and I sat down on our old settee on a Friday night to taste it. It was crisp, and light. It filled my mouth with the promise of high Canadian mountains and wide skies that rolled on and on. After another glass I was paddling in a rough canoe across a lake as still as a mirror; another glass and I felt I was approaching, as if by express train, some fundamental truth about Canada. Another glass and I devoured a family bag of crisps. Another glass and I just had to go to bed, despite the fact that it was still very early, well before the nine o'clock watershed, and I stood at the bottom of the stairs, waving to my wife and kids in what I told them was a traditional Canadian way, before stumbling into bed and into a deep abyss of sleep.

I woke up at 3 am, and I appeared to have become a piece of Arctic tundra from the very Northern tip of Canada's furthest reaches. I wandered downstairs, fending off the feeling that my head was somehow flapping like the outstretched wings of a Canada goose. In the back room I clicked the light on and both gerbils stirred in their cage, gazing around them with their noses through the straw. I realised that the sudden, unaccustomed light at 3 am had fooled them into thinking it was Saturday morning. I turned the light off, and the gerbils settled down, believing it to be Saturday night. I turned the light on again, and their little heads appeared, with Sunday morning looks on their faces. I clicked it off and they went back to sleep.

I surged with power; I thought of me flashing the lights on and off for hours like someone from Wells's *The Time Machine* as the gerbils steamed towards pensionable age. Then I was seized by guilt. What a terrible thing to contemplate doing. I was worse than the worst factory farmer. The gerbils thought it was Sunday night. I left them in the dark and tiptoed back to bed.

The next morning I felt clean and refreshed but the kids were gathered round the gerbils' cage like relatives at the scene of a pit disaster. One of the gerbils was breathing rapidly and its eyes were shut and its fur was matted with sweat. We took it to the vet as my guilt boiled inside me, and the vet injected it with a syringe at least one-and-a-half gerbils long. 'This'll liven it up,' he said. It didn't. The gerbil got worse. The vet said it was a lung infection and injected it with a syringe as big as a wine bottle. At home I sulked and people asked me what was wrong. I talked about the old straw, about how the gerbil could maybe pick up an infection from the old straw. I drank strong tea and left my cardboard box of Canadian wine alone. Two days later the gerbil died and there was a simple ceremony in the back garden, near the shed. My son made a small plaque with his Real Power Workshop and wrote on it with a felt tip: BUBBLE RIP. 2 YEARS OLD. Through fear I kept quiet. The other gerbil pined for its mate. It could have been the old straw, I guess, or it could have been the time of year. But I know it was my fault. Me and the crisp Canadian.

Insight: Five Ridiculous Old Yorkshire Sayings About Glasses

1.   You can't see the Moon without glasses,
But who knows what glasses the moon wears?

2.   Break your glasses and weep for a week,
Although you won't be able to find your hanky.

3.   Adam and Eve didn't need glasses.
Not at first.

4.   You can't carry anything in your glasses.
Except your eyes.

5.   Sandwiches have to be a certain shape
to fit in your glasses case.
And so do glasses.

Ancient Glasses Weather Lore

Glasses wet,
it's raining.
Glasses broke,
it's hailing.
Wipe your glasses,
It's foggy.
Mist makes your glasses
soggy.

Heyop. All right. That should be enough for a column. I shouldn't need to write any more, because I'm a South Yorkshireman, and we don't talk very much. Don't ask me why that is, it could be all those years of bad industrial news, all those years of pits shutting and steelworks locking their gates, all those years of standing at bus stops with little papers under our arms and cheese sandwiches in our bags.

Heyop. All right. It's not enough for me, I'm afraid. I've got to say more. I talk for a living, and that's what makes me an unusual South Yorkshireman. You can count us on the fingers of one hand, South Yorkshiremen who rattle for their supper: there's me, and Brian Glover, and Michael Parkinson and, now that he's retired, Dickie Bird. All the rest of them are South Yorkshire Minimalists, grunting and chuntering their way through life, never using more words than are absolutely necessary, from the cradle to the . . . you know.

I was in the barbers the other day; the room was full of South Yorkshiremen, so there was complete silence. A man stuck his head round the door. AR? he said. NO said the barber. REYT said the man. Loosely translated, that would read 'Hello, barber, I wonder if you could fit me in before half past five?' 'No sir, as you can see I've got a shop full.' 'Oh, all right then, I'll call back later.' Ar. No. Reyt. After I'd been to the barbers, I went to the chip shop, because I live life at the giddy limit. The shop was full of South Yorkshire people, so the only noise was the sizzling of the chips. The language in the chip shop was so minimal it was an opera by Steve Reich called The Chip Shop. It was a low calling out of numbers. TWICE. ONCE. TWICE AND A TAIL. In other words fish and chips twice, fish and chips once, fish and chips with a fishtail, but why waste words when there's been no good tidings in your town since Clement Attlee's day, and that was only temporary?

Sometimes words fail the South Yorkshire minimalists, and they have to resort to sounds, to cries and moans of existential pain and spiritual anguish. Eeee. I'm talking here about Eee, the universal indicator of the health of the South Yorkshire minimalist's soulcase. If you haven't heard soulcase before, it's where your soul lives. Obvious really.

So if a South Yorkshire man burns his hand he turns to the ceiling or heaven and says 'Eee'. If a South Yorkshire woman opens the newspaper and reads of some terrible disaster far away she folds the paper as though she's folding a towel and she says 'Eee', as the newspaper crackles.

There are two basic problems with South Yorkshire Minimalism; one is that it can't be translated into art. I once wrote a play about pigeon fanciers and I tried to make the language as close to the real South Yorkshire as I could. It worked in Barnsley. The tiny nuggets of language and sound got the desired effect. At Dodworth Miners Welfare the actors had to pause between lines for long minutes to let the audience stop laughing and get its breath back; in Worksop, which is just over the border in North Nottinghamshire, we may as well have been reading Goethe for all the laughs we got.

The other problem, and it's the main problem, is that if you're a South Yorkshire Minimalist you can express yourself too well. Declarations of love are stumbling, creaking, tearful things, and philosophy is a shrug rather than a discourse. I ER THAT KNOWS I ER LOVE THEE. Or THA KNOWS ITS LIKE HEID-EGGER SAYS . . .

I'm not offering solutions, though, I'm just pointing out the problem. I'm a linguistic exile, chattering away in a land of silent types. Listen to me, rattling on. Why don't I just shut up? Heuop. All right. See you. That should be enough for a column. More than enough. You could make ten columns out of all these words, aye, and still have change for a comment on the weather.

Happiness on the First Train
from Barnsley to Huddersfield

The happiness creeps up on you,
in the dark train as we stop at Dodworth,

then Silkstone Common, then Penistone,
and some people are sleeping and sleeping

is a sort of happiness, and those three men
who are always on this train are talking

and talking is a form of happiness, and I
am looking, and looking is a kind of

happiness. Then the train pulls out
of Penistone Station, across that impossibly

beautiful viaduct that I can never
remember the name of, and the light

is arriving in the sky as if by slow train,
and now I can remember the name

of the viaduct and the name
of the viaduct is Happiness,

Happiness high across the slowly
lightening fields.

Drains

Civilisation isn't really about huge thoughts bursting from the high foreheads of great thinkers, or buildings that appear to touch the sky and whose windows reflect the golden sunset a thousand winking times. Civilisation is about almost-hidden things, things that grease the wheel and help us stagger from one day to the next. Things like hatstands, toothpaste, and doors that lock. Things like scarves. Things like drains.

Drains somehow keep us human, keep us clean, keep us free from disease as the dishwasher gurgles and the toilet flushes. The oblong metal drain cover in the middle of the path is an emblem: here we are, human, greater than the flea or the turtle. I know this because I've been there when civilisation begins to crumble, when the map begins to singe at the edges and the hordes rattle at the locked door.

Our drains got blocked. We'd been away for a couple of days to a hotel with a pool and room service and we got back, feeling like a golden family, people to whom good things happen, and we noticed The Slime seeping out from under the cover. We got out of the car and the stench came up and slapped us, briskly. Images of the hotel and the pool and the room service and the fridge full of drinks faded as The Slime lapped around our feet. We retreated to the house. I felt it was like the end of the world, a plague, a pestilence. I felt the thin bubble of civilisation stretching to bursting point. My wife flicked through the yellow pages. She found a number and rang it. 'He'll be here in twenty minutes,' she said, and I felt reassured, felt civilisation returning to my body like colour does to your cheeks.

In an hour we rang again. He was on his way. In another hour we rang again. He was almost turning up the drive. In another forty-five minutes he turned up, in a white van with big, important writing on the side. I felt that I was learning things about civilisation, that when the crumbling starts you have to wait for a while for salvation, but when the help turns up it will at least look imposing.

The Drain Man climbed out. He was tall, thin, pasty. His hair was red, but not red like Mick Hucknall's: red like those bits of carrot you always find at the bottom of the sink. He had a little girl with him. 'My daughter,' he explained. 'She often comes out with me; finds it interesting, like.' He put on rubber gloves like a surgeon might, heaved the top off the drains, and looked inside with the aid of a powerful torch. He shook his head. 'We'll have to get the camera down,' he said, with an air of great sorrow.

And so it was that as the night darkened, a casual walker past my house would have seen a strange scene, a scene somehow redolent of Britain in the '90s, somehow indicative of the rush towards the millennium. A tall thin man in surgeon's gloves was poking a camera on the end of a long tube down a drain in the middle of a path. The tall man's daughter, and an entire family of people who had recently returned from a weekend in a posh hotel, were gazing, transfixed, at a small black-and-white TV monitor; the picture was of a drain, blocked. Every so often the man with red hair would say 'Roots' and his daughter would say 'Roots' and the family with the posh hotel's soap in their toilet bags would say 'Roots'.

He spent ages prodding that camera down that drain. I talked to him as the night thickened; he came from a small town in North Yorkshire, about seventy miles away from us in Barnsley. We were his tenth job of the day and he wouldn't get home until well past midnight. He was self employed, the gaffer preferred it that way, and he'd be at it again tomorrow. It was interesting work, especially when you got the camera out. It was good to have a job, these days. I gazed at the inside of my street, lit up on a tiny black and white screen, and I thought about civilisation, about how odd little things made us better than the flea or the turtle. 'Of course,' he said, 'I couldn't do it without the gloves. It'd be impossible without the gloves.' Like I said, civilisation's in the small things.

Some Lies and Some Truths about
Uncle Charlie and Jumping Crackers

Uncle Charlie loved Jumping Crackers so much
he used to spread them on toast. Uncle Charlie
had bad dreams about the War, and

Jumping Crackers make them come true. Uncle Charlie
is making a wire and concrete sculpture
of a Jumping Cracker in his back yard. Uncle

Charlie once got a Jumping Cracker
caught in the flaps of his trousers. Uncle Charlie
would whistle 'You're my Jumping

Cracker' during idle moments at the pit.
Uncle Charlie enjoys the roast
potatoes and the parkin, the bonfire

toffee and the hot dogs, the mugs
of hot tea with a drop in,
much more than he enjoys the Jumping Crackers.

The way the kids clamour for pets. The way the kids shout and weep for pets. The way the kids won't do their homework and won't go to their ballet class and won't do their clarinet lesson because they want pets. The way the mother and father look out of the window, thinking about peaceful times. The way the mother and father talk in hushed tones about the time before they had children. The way the mother and father see the time before they had children as a time suffused with a golden light and a smooth silence.

The way the kids clamour for pets. The way they get pet care books out of the library and read them with angelic looks on their faces before falling into deep, innocent and dreamless sleep. The way the kids watch *Wildlife on One* with wistful eyes. The way the kids watch *Animal Hospital* with wistful eyes. The way the kids linger at the windows of pet shops with faces full of infinite long-ing and Christlike acceptance of suffering. The way the parents lie in bed talking about pets. The way the parents like in bed talking about pets night after night. The way the parents talk about pets instead of having sex.

The way the kids clamour for pets. The way the debate hap-pens all the time. The way the visit to the grandmother is centred around her cat. The way the visit to the ordinary uncle is centred around his goldfish. The way the visit to the eccentric uncle is centred around his stick insects. The way the grandmother's cat purrs prettily. The way the ordinary uncle's goldfish goes O prettily. The way the eccentric uncle's stick insects sit there look-ing like sticks prettily. The way the visit to the garden-centre-cum-pet-shop is seen as a breach in the parents' defences. The way the visit to the garden-centre-cum-pet-shop is punctuated by cries of ooh and aaah. The way the kids won't eat their tea. The way their favourite video fails to make them laugh. The way the kids complain that they can't sleep. The way the kids stroke cuddly toys and hold cushions.

The way the kids clamour for pets. The way the parents begin to bicker. The way the parents bicker a lot. The way one parent thinks about the lovely little rabbit he had as a child. The way he recalls that it was called Bunny Fluff. The way one parent thinks about the lovely little dog she had as a child. The way she recalls that it was called Trixie. The way the parents begin to think of their childhood as a time wrapped in a love of pets. The way the parents think of their childhood as a time punctuated by barks, happy laughter, and the sound of a rabbit nibbling a carrot. The way both parents are coming round to the idea of pets separately but daren't tell the other parent. The way the parents talk about pets instead of having sex.

The way the kids clamour for pets. The way there is no laughter in the house anymore. The way the house is like a house in which there has been recent tragic news. The way the parents begin to lose concentration and lock keys in the car and forget to post important letters. The way the parents resolve to say at breakfast that the kids can have pets. The way the family sits around the breakfast table. The way the kids are leafing through wildlife magazines and reading books about pets who save families from barn fires. The way one parent clears his throat. The way one parent clears her throat.

The way the kids clamour for pets. The way both parents say at once ALL RIGHT THEN YOU CAN HAVE PETS. The way the kids do not react with joy. The way the kids react with a kind of quiet satisfaction. The way the parents are disappointed. The way the kids are secretly a little disappointed because the clamouring was fun.

The way the kids sit in the back of the car like little angels. The way the pet shop approaches like The Shining City on the Hill. The way one child says 'So we're getting a rabbit then.' The way one child says 'So we're getting a cat then.' The way one child says 'So we're getting a goldfish then.' The way the pet shop is getting nearer. The way the children's eyes gleam. The way the real clamouring can now begin. The way the real clamouring begins.

Minimal Yorkshire Pudding
River Songs

1. Waves like batter!
   Do you recall
   When the moon was the colour
   Of batter?

2. I can feel you, trout!
   I can feel you, trout!
   I can feel you, trout!
   Nudging me underneath . . .

3. I am a time travelling
   Yorkshire Pudding
   I am a handful of flour
   I am an egg
   I am some milk

   I am a time travelling
   River
   I am some water
   I am some fish
   I am some riverbank

4. Only the faintest of splashes
   Only the smallest of ripples
   Only the faintest of splashes
   Only the smallest of ripples

What to Wear

Well, you just don't know what to wear, do you? You just don't know what to put on. It's the weather. You just can't rely on it. This time of year you should at least be able to loosen a couple of buttons on your cardigan but the wind's blowing straight from Russia via Broomhill Flash and the showers we're getting are like those squalls they get in films about heroic fishermen. It's a good time to go Inappropriate Summer Clothing spotting, though. You can get points for all of these: spot every one and have hours of fun!

The white flat cap or white trilby. The straw benjy. The white flat cap fastened on with elastic (you might not believe this one, but I've seen it at least twice struggling up Market Hill). The white flat cap under the rainmate. The rainmate. The very old rainmate with holes in it. The headscarf on a very hot day. The headscarf in a paisley pattern on a very hot day. The headscarf with Views of Bridlington or Recipes for Bread on it on a very hot day. The old woman's chapel hat on a very hot day. The old woman's chapel hat held down with an old rainmate on a very hot day. (Extra points if the old woman is dabbing her brow with a tissue and saying to her mate, 'By, it's not just red hot: it's white hot.' Extra points if bits of tissue stick to the old woman's head like Forehead Dandruff.) The heavy tweed jacket. The heavy tweed jacket with waistcoat. The heavy tweed jacket with waistcoat and polo neck. The heavy tweed jacket with waistcoat and polo neck combined with the white flat cap fastened on with elastic (a high number of points for this one!) The heavy tweed jacket with raincoat carried over the arm. The heavy tweed jacket with raincoat carried over the arm and umbrella poking from the shopping basket. The sunglasses under the white flat cap held on with elastic. The sunglasses on top of the ordinary glasses. The sunglasses on the forehead, the ordinary glasses on the eyes. Vice versa. The tightly fitting male shirt (good time to spot these next few is on office lunch breaks). The tightly fitting male shirt with Comedy Tie. The tightly fitting male shirt with Comedy Bow Tie below sweating face with forehead dandruff. The tightly fitting male shirt with loosened tie and with pens in the top pocket one of which has burst making interesting blue patterns on the shirt. The short shorts. The long shorts. The shorts that should have been sent to the jumble sale. The shorts that were bought at a jumble sale. The denim shorts with tightly fitting male shirt, comedy bow tie and white flat cap held on with elastic. The sandals. The sandals with socks. The sandals with comedy socks (i.e. Bugs Bunny, Homer Simpson) as though the wearing of comedy socks somehow makes it okay. The boots with shorts. The wellies with shorts. The wellies with shorts and white flat cap held on with elastic. The T-shirt that fitted once, many years ago. The T-shirt that never fitted. The T-shirt with inappropriate slogan (Daventry, the Natural Centre for Business; I'm a Crazy Love Machine; Wilson's Red and White Army; My Parents Went to Humberston and all they Came Back with Was this Lousy T-Shirt and a White Flat Cap and Some Elastic, etc.) The mac. The parka with shorts and sandals. The parka with hood up, shorts, sandals, comedy socks and white flat cap held on with elastic.

Spot them all over the next few weeks of Summer and win a prize. You never know what to wear, do you? Does anybody know where I can get the elastic renewed on my white flat cap?

Free Improvising Musician Drops Frying Pan

Crash of it so random, depends
on all sorts: type of floor. Type
of frying pan. Position of the bacon and the eggs.

I'll incorporate it into the gig tonight,
somehow. Filtered through the day, of course,
the things I haven't done yet,

sounds I've not heard. Tonight's music
starts now, nice and early, this morning,
frying pan in mid air really the start of it,

start of all improvisation, the music
not yet heard, the bacon not yet

in a pattern on the floor, the eggs
running, running to keep up

with themselves. Keeping up with itself:
the music not yet played, not yet heard.

I Woke Up This Morning

For years I've said that writers and readers should make them-
selves Available for Experience: in other words they should
always be in a state of readiness for the words, or the image, or
the overhearing, or the sentence in a book, that might come their
way. It's a case of being mentally fit in the same way that an
athlete has to be physically fit, and it takes lots of practice in the
same way that physical fitness (so I'm told!) does.

Observation becomes second nature to a writer, as does
making connections between observations, and I've tried to take
this one step further by placing myself in positions where I'm
bound to observe stuff that might come into poems later. So the
other day I found myself on Bolton station with two and a half
hours to kill before a reading; the organiser had told me that if I
was early at the station I could go to his house for tea, but
although I would have enjoyed that, I knew that a few hours on
the station would be valuable for honing the observation muscles.

I saw lots of things and filed them away for future use: the
look on a fat man's face when he just missed his train after run-
ning like mad for it; the sandwich that I bought that said Ham on
the label but turned out to be tuna; the man who said into his
mobile 'phone 'I'll be in the air for most of tomorrow' which is a
great line for a poem, and the way that the tannoy from the
factory opposite the station kept mixing with the station
announcer to form an interesting wordscape. As I sat there I
wondered if you could actually make things happen just by sit-
ting there, and I sat there for a bit and nothing happened, but I
didn't really mind because my observation bank had been filled
up to the very top.

And then a strange thing happened, and you'll probably think
I'm making it up but all I can tell you is that I'm not and you'll
have to believe me. The next day, back at home, I put my coat on
to go out and I felt in the pocket and there, to my absolute sur-
prise, was a harmonica, a little one like blues players play, and
I've absolutely no idea how it got there. I haven't got a harmonica,
and none of my kids have got a harmonica and I don't know any-
body who owns a harmonica. Except me, now. And all I can

94

think is that somebody slipped it into my pocket as I sat on Bolton station being Available for Experience. The opposite of a harmonica thief passed by and now I'm one harmonica richer, which is pretty poetic, don't you think?

And I'm sure I'll write a poem about it soon, and I'll do my best not to make the harmonica into some kind of heavy-handed symbol for anything. It shines well enough just as it is, and it sounds really lovely.